$\mathcal{A}$DVENT *and* $\mathcal{C}$HRISTMAS $\mathcal{W}$ISDOM

from

SAINT THOMAS AQUINAS

Advent and Christmas Wisdom

from

SAINT THOMAS AQUINAS

Daily Scripture and Prayers
Together With
Saint Thomas Aquinas's Own Words

Compiled by Andrew Carl Wisdom, OP

Liguori
LIGUORI, MISSOURI

Imprimi Potest:
Thomas D. Picton, C.Ss.R.
Provincial, Denver Province
The Redemptorists

Published by Liguori
Liguori, Missouri
To order, call 800-325-9521
www.liguori.org

Library of Congress Cataloging-in-Publication Data
Thomas, Aquinas, Saint, 1225?-1274.
  Advent and Christmas wisdom from St. Thomas Aquinas / compiled by Andrew Carl Wisdom. -- 1st ed.
      p. cm.
  ISBN 978-0-7648-1819-6
  1. Advent--Prayers and devotions. 2. Christmas--Prayers and devotions. 3. Thomas, Aquinas, Saint, 1225?-1274--Quotations. I. Wisdom, Andrew-Carl, 1961- II. Title.
  BV40.T46 2009
  242'.33--dc22

                                                        2009017850

Acknowledgments of sources of quotations from Saint Thomas Aquinas are listed on p. 115.

Printed in the United States of America
First edition
13 12 11 10 09   5 4 3 2 1

Contents

Introduction

WHEN PEOPLE HEAR THE NAME Saint Thomas Aquinas, OP, they might conjure up an intimidating image of a ponderous, theological know-it-all who has an answer for everything. Certainly some have approached him in this way. But this picture of Aquinas does a disservice to him and to the Church he so zealously loved, nurtured, and defended.

I would invite another reading altogether. Thomas's spirit was characteristically one of being in conversation with God, himself, and the world, allowing the truth of things to surface out of that dynamic exchange. His instinct was not a knee-jerk appeal to authority but a careful search for the truth, respectfully weighing differing and sometimes opposing perspectives. For Aquinas, the starting and ending point were the same: the singular desire for God.

A popular story offers a fitting introduction to this spiritual and intellectual giant. Growing frustrated as he worked on the composition of a text on the Eucharist, Thomas stood before a crucifix and beseeched the Lord to render judgment. A voice said: "Thomas, you have written well of me. What would you like from me?"

"*Nil nisi te, Lord. Nil nisi te,*" Thomas replied. (Nothing but you, Lord. Nothing but you.) The desire that led to such an unparalleled output as a philosopher and theologian flowed from the religious commitment he had made as an obedient, generous, and compassionate Dominican friar. The living out of this desire made him more than simply one of the greatest and most creative minds in the history of Western civilization. Lifelong fidelity to the pursuit of his desire for God alone is what made him a saint, his greatest achievement.

Far from the dry scholastic that his formal style might suggest, Thomas was a deeply affective man, passionately and unequivocally in love with God. Thomas enjoyed an intimate relationship with God and sought to share it with others. It started as all great, enduring love affairs do, with a mysterious fascination upon being introduced to his future Beloved. As a small boy, Thomas surprised his Benedictine teachers again and again with the question: "But Master, what is God?"

To even begin to understand something of Aquinas, one has to appreciate the significance of this question as the one that ceaselessly haunted him throughout his life. This profound inquiry of the heart gave shape to Thomas's Herculean output as both teacher and scholar and defines his remarkable and unprecedented legacy. It would become the defining purpose of his life: striving to describe who and what God is, and spending his life sharing that discovery with others through his preaching, teaching, and writing in the Dominican tradition.

Born the youngest of ten children in a well-to-do family at their castle near Aquino (between Rome and Naples) around the year 1225, Thomas was sent, at the age of five, to the Benedictine monastery at Monte Cassino. There he would be educated by the monks and, it was assumed, would one day rise to the prestigious position of abbot. At least this was the hope of his mother, Theodora, and his father, Landulf, a minor nobleman. But Thomas had other ideas.

After nine years, Thomas left the abbey in 1239 to take up

undergraduate studies at the University of Naples where he was exposed to the newly discovered thought of the Greek philosopher, Aristotle. This would have a lasting and, for his detractors, unfortunate influence on him. At the university in 1243, Thomas met a new and exciting "ragtag" group of wandering religious known as the friar preachers and stunned his family by joining them. A generation before, a charismatic Spaniard named Saint Dominic de Guzman had gathered a band of preachers around him to respond to the spread of heresy and to promote a true understanding of the Catholic faith.

What captivated Thomas about the Dominicans was the attractive integration of a monastic rhythm of life, as he had known and loved it with the Benedictines, and a mission to the world that was concrete, active, and compelling. Contrary to anything the world had seen at that point, these white and black-robed friars traveled the highways and byways, living hand-to-mouth and holding all things in common like the early Apostles and, like the Apostles, preaching the Good News to all they met. The apostolic life of preaching for the salvation of souls proved too much for Thomas to resist. He joined the friars in 1244, a decision G. K. Chesterton said was akin to running away and "[marrying] a gypsy."

The years from 1245 to 1273 saw Thomas, ever the generous, obedient friar, moving in response to his Order's needs and traveling between Paris, Cologne, Rome, and Naples. In Cologne, his intellectual collaboration and friendship with Saint Albert the Great, OP, had its genesis. Albert made his famous prediction of "the dumb ox" (as his classmates called the shy, quiet student with the big six-foot frame): "You call him the Dumb Ox; I tell you this Dumb Ox shall bellow so loud that his bellowings will fill the world."

On December 6, 1273, Thomas had just finished celebrating Mass on the Feast of Saint Nicholas when he had a mysterious, religious experience after which he stopped all of his writing and teaching. When his friend Reginald asked him why, Thomas simply explained: "Reginald, everything that I have written seems like so much straw compared to what has been revealed to me."

Three months and a day after that event, Thomas died, but not before one final confession and act of faith. After receiving Communion, he prayed: "I am receiving thee, Price of my soul's redemption: all my studies, my vigils, and my labors have been for love of thee. I have taught much and written much of the most sacred body, O Jesus Christ; I have taught and written in the faith of Jesus Christ and the holy Roman Church, to whose judgment I offer and submit everything."

Pope John XXII canonized Thomas in 1323. Two hundred and forty-four years later, he was declared a doctor of the Church by Pope Pius V, himself a Dominican. Finally, in 1880, Pope Leo XIII appointed "the angelic doctor," as Thomas became affectionately known, patron of all Catholic universities.

These selections from Thomas's inspirational works will show him to be a practical spiritual guide and accessible spiritual director of the first order, as well as a noted scriptural commentator, poet, mystic, and philosopher. They are drawn from his works: *Commentary on the Gospel of St. John*, *Sermon on the Apostles' Creed*, *The Three Greatest Prayers*, *Commentaries on the Commandments and Sacraments* (*God's Greatest Gifts*), and *The Compendium of Theology*, a synopsis of his masterpiece, *Summa Theologiae*, which is also referenced extensively. This last work was Thomas's greatest contribution, because while other theologians stitched together helpful opinions to explain a theological issue, Thomas, in the *Summa*, went further in weaving a rich tapestry of the whole. For him, these interconnecting threads weave a magnificent picture of a Creator who loves us with lavish abundance and who wants a dynamic relationship with us best likened to intimate human friendship. We are not merely God's sons and daughters; we are destined to be his beloved friends. God wants us to know that he is our deepest truth and that all the goods in the world are for our enjoyment as long as they lead us to him.

Aquinas has been the subject of many artists who generally show him in various postures of study, happily besieged by his beloved books. But Father Robert Staes, OP, offers an artistic rendering of Thomas that is as unprecedented as it is provocative. It is also the one I want to offer you as we begin this liturgical season brimming with hope-filled anticipation. It captures Thomas at the time of his mystical revelation, not pushing away his pen and books, but up on his feet, waving straw in both hands, dancing as though deliriously happy at what has been revealed to him. May we who walk through Advent and Christmas know something of that same dizzying delight!

HOW TO USE THIS BOOK

Advent—that period of great anticipatory joy—is a time of preparation for the celebration of Christ's arrival in Bethlehem as a helpless infant. In the Western liturgy, Advent begins four Sundays prior to December 25—the Sunday closest to November 30, which is the feast of Saint Andrew, one of Jesus' first disciples.

The annual commemoration of Christ's birth begins the Christmas cycle of the liturgical year—a cycle that runs from Christmas Eve to the Sunday after the feast of the Epiphany. In keeping with the unfolding of the message of the liturgical year, this book is designed to be used during the entire period from the first Sunday of Advent to the end of the Christmas cycle.

The four weeks of Advent are often thought of as symbolizing the four different ways that Christ comes into the world: (1) at his birth as a helpless infant in Bethlehem; (2) at his arrival in the hearts of believers; (3) at his death; and (4) at his arrival on Judgment Day.

Because Christmas falls on a different day of the week each year, the fourth week of Advent is never really finished; it is abruptly, joyously, and solemnly abrogated by the annual coming again of Christ at Christmas. Christ's Second Coming will also one day abruptly interrupt our sojourn here on earth.

Since the calendar dictates the number of days in Advent, this book includes Scripture quotations and meditative excerpts from the writings of Saint Thomas Aquinas for twenty-eight days. The daily readings make up Part I of this book. The reader may want to begin with Part I and, on Christmas Day, switch to Part II, which contains materials for the twelve days of Christmas. If there are any "extra" entries from Part I, these may be read by doubling up days or by reading two entries on weekends. Alternately, one may just skip those entries that do not fit within the Advent time frame for that particular year.

Each "day" in this book begins with the words of Saint Thomas Aquinas. Following that quotation is an excerpt from Scripture that is related in some way. Next is a prayer, also built on the ideas from the two preceding passages. Finally, an Advent or Christmas "action" is suggested as a way to apply the messages to one's daily life. A prayer meditation is offered on page 113 to read morning or evening before reflecting on Saint Thomas Aquinas's words each day.

PART I
~~~~~~~~~

READINGS FOR ADVENT

DAY 1

*T*he first point about eternal life is that man is united with God. For God himself is the reward and end of all our labors: *I am your protector and your supreme reward.* This union consists in seeing perfectly: *At present we are looking at a confused reflection in a mirror, but then we shall see face to face.*

Next it consists in perfect praise, according to the words of the prophet: *Joy and happiness will be found in it, thanksgiving and words of praise.*

It also consists in the complete satisfaction of desire, for there the blessed will be given more than they wanted or hoped for. The reason is that in this life no one can fulfill his longing, nor can any creature satisfy man's desire. Only God satisfies, he infinitely exceeds all other pleasures. That is why man can rest in nothing but God. As Augustine says: *You have made us for yourself, Lord, and our heart can find no rest until it rests in you.*

CREDO IN DEUM: OPUSCULA THEOLOGICA 2
SERMON ON THE APOSTLES' CREED

Be patient, therefore, brothers, until the coming of the Lord. See how the farmer waits for the precious fruit of the earth, being patient with it until it receives the early and the late rains. You too must be patient. Make your hearts firm, because the coming of the Lord is at hand.

JAMES 5:7–8

PRAYER

Gracious God, why do I have to learn this lesson over and over again: to wait for you, that my heart will not rest until it rests in you? Since the moment of my conception, I was destined for union with you. That's why nothing and no one else can ultimately satisfy me. Unite my heart this day to yours that I may patiently rest in the lesson learned of your peace and grace. May my daily life mirror its promise of you.

ADVENT ACTION

Advent is a time of patient waiting for the Lord to be reborn once again in our hearts. Today, identify two or three of the most common issues you wrestle with that continually hinder restful, patient waiting. Write them down and tape them to your mirror. This will remind you of your personal roadblocks to a peaceful union of your heart with God's each day.

DAY 2

*T*he reason why we must hope in God is chiefly the fact that we belong to Him, as effect belongs to cause. God does nothing in vain, but always acts for a definite purpose....

A cause that operates intellectually not only confers on the effect, in the act of producing it, all that is required for the result intended, but also, when the product is finished, controls its use, which is the end of the object. Thus a smith, in addition to forging a knife, has the disposition of its cutting efficiency. Man is made by God somewhat as an article is made by an artificer. Something of this sort is said in Isaiah 64:8: "And now, O LORD, Thou art our Father and we are clay, and Thou art our Maker."

Accordingly, just as an earthen vessel, if it were endowed with sense, might hope to be put to good use by the potter, so man ought to cherish the hope of being rightly provided for by God. Thus we are told in Jeremiah 18:6: "As clay is in the hand of the potter, so are you in my hand, O house of Israel."

LIGHT OF FAITH: THE COMPENDIUM OF THEOLOGY

For I know well the plans I have in mind for you, says the LORD, plans for your welfare, not for woe! Plans to give you a future full of hope. When you call me, when you go to pray to me, I will listen to you. When you look for me, you will find me. Yes, when you seek me with all your heart, you will find me with you, says the LORD, and I will change your lot…

JEREMIAH 29:11–14

PRAYER

God of hope, I belong to you. I was not made in vain. As clay in your gentle hands, form me into something beautiful and unique for you. Send me out for your holy purposes. Direct this earthen vessel of your making toward only that which fulfills your purpose in, through, and with me.

ADVENT ACTION

With gentle heart and hands, can you imbue others with hope? Today, monitor your thoughts, words, and gestures to avoid catering to the cultural cynicism so often found at the water cooler. Instead, be a "herald of hope" at the breakfast table, in the lunch line, or at the company dinner meeting.

DAY 3

*T*his kingdom is desirable because of its perfect liberty.... all shall be of one will with God: whatever the saints will, God shall will; and whatever God wills, the saints shall will. Therefore, their will shall be done with God's will. In this way, all will reign, since the will of all will be done, and God shall be the crown of all: "In that day shall the Lord of hosts be for a crown of glory and for a diadem of beauty unto the residue of His people."

This kingdom is also desirable because of its wondrous wealth: "The eye hath not seen, O God, besides Thee, what things Thou has prepared for them that wait on Thee." "Who satisfieth thy desire with good things."

Take note that whatever man seeks in this world, he will find it more perfect and more excellent in God alone. If you seek delight, you will find supreme delight in God: "You shall see and your hearts shall rejoice." "And everlasting joy shall be upon your heads." Do you seek wealth? You will find in Him all things you desire in abundance: "When the soul strays from Thee she seeks things apart from Thee, but finds all things impure and unprofitable until she returns to Thee."

THE THREE GREATEST PRAYERS

But our citizenship is in heaven, and from it we also await a savior, the Lord Jesus Christ.

He will change our lowly body to conform with his glorified body by the power that enables him also to bring all things into subjection to himself.

PHILIPPIANS 3:20–21

PRAYER

Loving God, I don't like to wait. So I don't wait to see the unfolding of your kingdom or to rejoice in the Savior you have given me, because I would have to relinquish control. Too often I end up creating *my* kingdom rather than turning to *thy* kingdom. Impatient, I stray from your presence, grasping at things and people rather than letting you alone satisfy my deepest desires. You see, Lord, if I am really honest, while I believe in you, I don't always trust that you will be there to pick up the pieces. This Advent, make my will one with yours so that I may put greater trust in true wealth—your saving presence—especially on the days when mine feels so impoverished.

ADVENT ACTION

Instead of being impatient when you are waiting somewhere today, whether in traffic, the grocery line, or the doctor's office, say a prayer for the person in front of you.

DAY 4

*T*he Son of God is nothing else but the Word of God, not like the word that is uttered externally (for this is transitory) but as the word conceived inwardly. Therefore this same Word of God is of one nature with God and equal to God....

We ought to be willing to hear God's words....to believe God's words....The Word of God abiding in us should be continually in our thoughts....We ought to communicate God's Word to others by admonishing them, preaching to them, and inflaming their hearts....We ought to put God's Word into practice: "Be ye doers of the Word and not hearers only, deceiving yourselves."

THE THREE GREATEST PRAYERS

What was from the beginning,
what we have heard,
what we have seen with our eyes,
what we looked upon
and touched with our hands
concerns the Word of life—
for the life was made visible;
we have seen it and testify to it
and proclaim to you the eternal life
that was with the Father and was made visible to us—
what we have seen and heard
we proclaim now to you,
so that you too may have fellowship with us;
for our fellowship is with the Father
and with his Son, Jesus Christ.
We are writing this so that our joy may be complete.

1 JOHN 1:1–3

PRAYER

God of light and love, let your Word be born in me, spoken through me, written upon my heart. In whatever way you speak to me today, may I be open to receiving your Word and not hesitate in believing your Word. May all my tasks today emanate from the power of your Word. May I share that Word in spoken and unspoken ways. It feels like a tall order, Father, but I never want to stop trying. Grant me the courage of my request and the grace to live its answer.

ADVENT ACTION

This morning, take a line from a psalm, hymn, or other prayer and memorize it. Use this line to bring yourself continually back to God's presence by repeating it quietly throughout the day during routine activities like driving, washing the dishes, or deleting emails.

DAY 5

*W*e should also bear in mind that, while Providence watches solicitously over all creatures, God exercises special care over rational beings. For the latter are exalted to the dignity of God's image and can rise to the knowledge and love of Him, and have dominion over their actions, since they are able to discriminate between good and evil. Hence, they should have confidence in God, not only that they may be preserved in existence in keeping with the condition of their nature…but that, by avoiding evil and doing good, they may merit some reward from him. We are taught a salutary lesson in Psalm 35:7: "Men and beasts Thou wilt preserve" (that is, God bestow on men and irrational creatures alike whatever pertains to the sustaining of life). And then the Psalmist adds, in the next verse: "But the children of men shall put their trust under the covert of Thy wings," indicating that they will be protected by God with special care.

LIGHT OF FAITH: THE COMPENDIUM OF THEOLOGY

Can a mother forget her infant,
     be without tenderness for the child of her womb?
Even should she forget,
     I will never forget you.
See, upon the palms of my hands,
     I have written your name;
     your walls are ever before me.
Your rebuilders make haste,
     as those who torn you down and laid you waste
     go forth from you;
Look about and see,
     they are all gathering and coming to you.
As I live says the LORD,
     you shall be arrayed with them all
     as with adornments,
     like a bride you shall fasten them on you.

ISAIAH 49:15–18

PRAYER

Gentle Father, I am under your care at all times and in all places and circumstances. There is not a moment of the day that I am not under your protection and loving gaze. You see and love in me what you see and love in your Son. You give me what I need to make choices that will lead me closer to you, as well as what I need to avoid false choices that take me away from you. May the confidence of your ever-present concern be at the center of all I do and say today.

ADVENT ACTION

Examine the recent pattern of your choices among people and with things, and note whether they have led you closer to God or made you feel more distant. Resolve to make today's choices with confidence, and trust in God's ever-present guidance in your life. Note whether these choices drew you toward God or away from him, whether they left you filled up or "on empty."

DAY 6

*A*ugustine [says], *As soon as charity is born it is fed*, a reference to beginners; *fed, it grows strong*, a reference to those making progress; *grown strong it becomes perfect*, which applies to the perfect. Accordingly there are three degrees of charity.

Some resemblances can be discerned between the spiritual growth of charity and a man's bodily growth. For even though many stages can be distinguished in the body's growth, there are certain clearly marked divisions...babyhood...[the] stage when he begins to talk...puberty...full manhood.

In the same way, various stages can be marked according as growth in charity leads a man to fix his main attention on different things. For, to begin with, he must devote himself mainly to withdrawing from sin and resisting the appetites, which drive him in the opposite direction to charity. This is the condition of beginners, who need to nourish and carefully foster charity to prevent it being lost. A second stage now follows, when a man's chief preoccupation is to advance in virtue. This is the mark of those who are making progress, and who are principally concerned that their charity should grow and become strong. The third stage is when a man applies himself chiefly to the work of cleaving to God and enjoying him, which is characteristic of the perfect who long to depart and be with Christ. [See Philippians 1:23.] We see the same kind of thing in the movement of a body, which first of all draws away from one point, then approaches, and finally comes to rest at another point.

SUMMA THEOLOGIAE

"'Lord, when did we see you hungry and feed you, or thirsty and give you drink? When did we see you a stranger and welcome you, or naked and clothe you? When did we see you ill or in prison, and visit you?' And the king will say to them in reply, 'Amen, I say to you, whatever you did for one of these least brothers of mine, you did for me.'"

MATTHEW 25:37–40

PRAYER

Loving Father, with the gift of your only Son, eternal charity was born into the world. Your divine mercy became incarnate in the hungry, the thirsty, the naked, and the stranger among us. This Advent help me to be free from all that drives me in the opposite direction of charity to my neighbor, so that I might be free for the claims of charity to which the most vulnerable invite us.

ADVENT ACTION

This liturgical season is a time of preparation for the coming of the Lord. Today, prepare your heart to receive wholeheartedly not just your friends and family, but the emotionally thirsty child, the poorly clothed stranger, and the spiritually hungry co-worker. Cleaving to God, be the divine charity they feed on today.

DAY 7

When any perfection is conferred, an ability to do or acquire something is also added. For example, when the air is illuminated by the sun, it has a capacity to serve as a medium for sight; and when water is heated by fire it can be used to cook—and it could hope for this if it had a mind. To man is given, over and above the nature of his soul, the perfection of grace, by which he is made a partaker in the divine nature....As a result of this, we are said to be regenerated and to become sons of God....Thus raised to be sons, men may reasonably hope for an inheritance, as we learn from Romans 8:17: "If sons, heirs also." In keeping with this spiritual regeneration, man should yet have a higher hope in God, namely, the hope of receiving an eternal inheritance.

LIGHT OF FAITH: THE COMPENDIUM OF THEOLOGY

I mean that as long as the heir is not of age, he is no different from a slave, although he is the owner of everything, but he is under the supervision of guardians and administrators until the date set by his father. In the same way we also, when we were not of age, were enslaved to the elemental powers of the world. But when the fullness of time had come, God sent his Son, born of a woman, born under the law, to ransom those under the law, so that we might receive adoption. As proof that you are children, God sent the spirit of his Son into our hearts, crying out: "Abba, Father!" So you are no longer a slave but a child, and if a child then also an heir, through God.

GALATIANS 4:1–7

PRAYER

Abba, Father, you sent your Son to announce the height, depth, and sheer breadth of your noble plan for our salvation. In showing your face to us, he revealed our identity as your sons and daughters. In this revelation, you ignite within me the fire of hope for that eternal inheritance promised to all your children: heirs of the grace to live in your presence forever where we will know no distance from you.

ADVENT ACTION

As the sun fulfills its natural purpose of being a medium of light, as fire provides the natural means of heating and warming water, fulfill your natural purpose as a means and medium of God's revelation of friendship. Truly listen patiently and sincerely to someone in distress today.

DAY 8

God came in the flesh so that the darkness might apprehend the light, i.e. obtain a knowledge of it. "The people who walked in darkness saw a great light" (Is 9:2)....

For the prophets came and John had come; but they were not able to give sufficient enlightenment, because **he was not the light**. And so, after the prophecies of the prophets and the coming of John, it was necessary that the light itself come and give the world a knowledge of itself. And this is what the Apostle says: "In past times, God spoke in many ways and degrees to our fathers through the prophets; in these days he has spoken to us in his Son."

For creatures were not sufficient to lead to a knowledge of the Creator....Thus it was necessary that the Creator himself come into the world in the flesh, and be known through himself. And this is what the Apostle says: "Since in the wisdom of God the world did not know God by its wisdom, it pleased God to save those who believe by the foolishness of our preaching" (1 Cor 1:21).

COMMENTARY ON THE GOSPEL OF ST. JOHN

He was in the world,

> *and the world came into being through him;*
> *but the world did not know him.*

He came to what was his own

> *but his own people did not accept him.*
>
> *But to those who did accept him he gave power to become* *children of God, to those who believe in his name, who were* *born not by natural generation nor by human choice nor by* *man's decision but of God.*

JOHN 1:10–13

PRAYER

Creator God, we come from, are made for, and are destined to be with YOU. Knowing this is true wisdom. Your Son, our divine light, came to proclaim that while we live in this world, we are citizens of another. Through the way I live, help me to be a walking, breathing preaching of another world, no matter how foolish it may seem to others.

ADVENT ACTION

Today, find three opportunities to share your faith, no matter how foolish or awkward it may feel. Consciously carry the image of being a walking, breathing preaching throughout your day to all you encounter.

DAY 9

Nothing is more like the Word of God than the unvoiced word that is conceived in man's heart. Now the word conceived in the heart is unknown to all except the one who conceives it; it is first known to others when the voice gives utterance it. Thus the Word of God while yet in the bosom of the Father was known to the Father alone; but when he was clothed with flesh as a word is clothed with the voice, then He was first made manifest and known: "Afterwards He was seen on earth and conversed with men."

…Another example lies in the fact that although the voiced word is known through hearing, it is not seen or touched; but when it is written, it is both seen and touched. In like manner, the Word of God became both visible and tangible when He was, as it were, written on our flesh.

Just as the parchment on which the king's word is written is called the king's word, so the man united to God's Word in unity of person is called the Word of God: "Take thee a great book and write in it with a man's pen." And therefore the holy Apostles said, *Who was conceived of the Holy Spirit and born of the Virgin Mary.*

THE THREE GREATEST PRAYERS

Therefore, brothers, since through the blood of Jesus we have confidence of entrance into the sanctuary by the new and living way he opened for us through the veil, that is, his flesh, and since we have "a great priest over the house of God," let us approach with a sincere heart and in absolute trust, with our hearts sprinkled clean from an evil conscience and our bodies washed in pure water. Let us hold unwaveringly to our confession that gives us hope, for he who has made the promise is trustworthy. We must consider how to rouse one another to love and good works.

HEBREWS 10:19–24

PRAYER

All powerful Father, the Word became clothed in flesh. Clothe me with that same Word. Give me the courage to enflesh the spoken and written Word of God today by what people hear me say and by what they see and touch in me. Beneath the veil of my choices made in the shadow of your presence, write upon the parchment of my life. With your pen, author a great book that gives utterance to faith's voice.

ADVENT ACTION

In what values do you daily clothe yourself? Is God present in your actions? Are you allowing God to write a great book in you? While veils hide things, they also allow us to penetrate their walls to the truth hidden in the shadows. The humanity of Jesus is the door through which we enter the sanctuary of God. Strive to let people enter the sanctuary of God through the veil of your humanity today, making the Word visible and tangible by what people see and touch of God in you.

DAY 10

The Holy Spirit saw that in the future some men would say that the world had always existed. "In the last days there shall come deceitful scoffers, walking after their own lusts, saying: 'Where is His promise or His coming? For since the time that the fathers slept, all things continue as they were from the beginning of creation.' For of this they are willfully ignorant, that the heavens existed long ago and the earth was formed out of water and through water by the word of God." God, therefore, wished that one day should be set aside in memory of the fact that He created all things in six days and that on the seventh day He rested from the creation of new creatures. This is why the Lord placed this Commandment in the Law, saying: *Remember that thou keep holy the Sabbath day....*

The Jews kept the Sabbath in memory of the first creation, but Christ at his coming brought about a new creation. For by the first creation an earthly man was created and by the second a heavenly man was formed....This new creation is through grace....

GOD'S GREATEST GIFTS

Thus say the Lord…
Remember not the events of the past,
*   the things of long ago consider not;*
See, I am doing something new!
*   Now it springs forth, do you not perceive it?*
In the desert, I make a way,
*   in the wastelands, rivers.*
The people whom I formed for myself,
*   that they might announce my praise.*
Yet you did not call upon me, O Jacob,
*   for you grew weary of me, O Israel.*
Instead, you burdened me with your sins,
*   and wearied me with your crimes.*
It is I, I who wipe out,
*   for my own sake, your offenses;*
*   your sins I remember no more.*

ISAIAH 43:16, 18–19, 21–22, 24B–25

PRAYER

Longed for Savior, in your birth is our hope in being formed anew from an earthly creation to heaven's sons and daughters. I now perceive who I was formed to be: the present announcement of God's praise. I am charged with setting aside one day each week to honor the person I have been created anew to be. Give me the discipline and the fortitude to stay awake to this truth, to live and act out of that sacred memory in each effort, event, and encounter of the other six days. Then my hope born in Christ's coming will be born in others, and my whole life will become a living Sabbath in Christ's memory.

ADVENT ACTION

How do you keep holy the Sabbath in memory of not just the first creation, but of the new creation that the coming of Christ accomplished in you? This week, set aside a morning or afternoon as time strictly for the Lord, to rekindle the memory of the new person the coming of Christ brought about in you and continues to bring about in you. On that day, spend time in prayer such as spiritual reading, praying the rosary, visiting a sacred place, or watching a movie with a religious theme.

DAY 11

We pray that *Thy kingdom come* because sometimes sin reigns in the world. This occurs when a man is so disposed that he follows at once the lure of sin and carries it into effect: "Let not sin reign in your mortal body" but let God reign in your heart ("who says to Zion, 'Thy God shall reign'"). This will be when you are ready to obey God and keep all His commandments. When therefore we ask that His kingdom may come, we pray that God (and not sin) may reign in us.

…[F]rom the moment that a man desires God to be Lord of all, he ceases to seek revenge for the injury done to himself and leaves that to God. For if you were to avenge yourself, you would no longer seek the advent of this kingdom.

…[I]f you await the coming of His kingdom, i.e. the glory of paradise, you have no need to regret the loss of earthly goods.

…[I]f you pray that God may reign in you, Christ Who was most meek also will reign in you.…

THE THREE GREATEST PRAYERS

Join with others in being imitators of me, brothers, and observe those who thus conduct themselves according to the model you have in us. For many, as I have often told you and now tell you even in tears, conduct themselves as enemies of the cross of Christ. Their end is destruction. Their God is their stomach; their glory is in their "shame." Their minds are occupied with earthy things. But our citizenship is in heaven, and from it we also await a savior, the Lord Jesus Christ. He will change our lowly bodies to conform with His glorified body by the power that enables him also to bring all things into subjection to himself.

PHILIPPIANS 3:17–21

PRAYER

Christ Jesus, I seek the advent of the kingdom in my own heart. For you told us that the kingdom is already within us and that all we seek can be found there. In this season of preparation, help me to await the deepening of that awareness of the kingdom within and all around me. Free my mind from preoccupation with earthly goods so that God may reign in me without competition.

ADVENT ACTION

Today, reflect on your stewardship of the goods God has given you in your life. Do they preoccupy you? Do they encourage your focus, not on material or earthly goods, but on the imperishable good of God's kingdom? Start with a good-size packing box and fill it with clothes and other items you are hanging on to that you don't need. Mark in big letters: "Outbox."

DAY 12

𝒥t is the Holy Spirit who gives this fortitude: "The Spirit entered into me…and He set me upon my feet." And this gift of fortitude prevents man's heart from fainting though fear of lacking necessities, and makes him trust without wavering that God will provide him with whatever he needs. For this reason the Holy Spirit, the giver of fortitude, teaches us to pray to God to *give us this day our daily bread.* For this reason, he is called the "Spirit of fortitude."

…There are some who are worried from day to day about temporal matters as much as a year in advance. Those who are so concerned are never at rest: "Be not solicitous, saying: 'What shall I eat?' or 'What shall we drink?' or 'What are we to put on?'" Hence our Lord teaches us to ask that our bread be given us *today,* i.e., whatever we need for the present.

…[W]e may discover in this bread another two-fold meaning: the Sacramental Bread and the Bread of God's Word.

…Thus, we ask for our Sacramental Bread which is prepared for us every day in the Church, praying that as we receive it sacramentally, so may it profit us unto salvation: "I am the living bread come down from heaven."

...Again this bread means the Word of God: "Not by bread alone doth man live but by every word that proceedeth from the mouth of God." Hence, we pray to Him to give us bread, that is to say, His Word. From this there arises in man the beatitude of hungering for righteousness, because the possession of spiritual goods increases our desire for them. This desire begets that hunger whose reward is the fullness of eternal life.

THE THREE GREATEST PRAYERS

So they said to him, "What can we do to accomplish the works of God?" Jesus answered and said to them, "This is the work of God, that you believe in the one he sent." So they said to him, "What sign can you do, that we may see and believe in you? What can you do? Our ancestors ate manna in the desert, as it is written: 'He gave them bread from heaven to eat.'" So Jesus said to them, "Amen, Amen, I say to you, it is not Moses who gave you the bread from heaven; my Father gives you the true bread from heaven. For the bread of God is that which comes down from heaven."

JOHN 6:28–32

PRAYER

Spirit of fortitude, you teach me to boldly and unapologetically turn to the living bread come down from heaven for what I need *today*. Give me the courage to not live in the past, which is already gone, or the future, which is not yet here. Rather, show me how to live in this present moment in which all that I need of God's love and grace is provided for me when I simply ask for it.

ADVENT ACTION

The majority of the people on the planet, some even in your own town or city, go to bed hungry every night. What can you do about the problem of hunger in the world? Consider collecting items from your kitchen and driving your gifts over to the local food pantry or church.

DAY 13

The incarnation was effective in delivering man from evil. First, for our instruction, lest we put the devil above ourselves and go in awe of him who is the author of sin. And so Augustine writes, *When human nature is so joined to God as to become one with him in person, these proud and evil spirits no longer dare to vaunt themselves over man because they are without flesh.*

Second, we are taught how great is the dignity of human nature, lest we sully it by sin. To the point Augustine writes, *God showed us the exalted place that human nature holds in creation by appearing to men as a true man.* So also Pope Leo, *O Christian, acknowledge your dignity; having been made a sharer of the divine nature, refuse to fall back into your previous worthlessness by your conduct.*

Third, to do away with human presumption *the grace of God, with no preceding merits on our part, is shown to us in the man Christ,* so Augustine writes.

Fourth, as he adds, *the pride of man, which is the greatest obstacle to our union with God, can be rebutted and cured by such great humility on the part of God.*

SUMMA THEOLOGIAE

Comfort, give comfort to my people, says your God.
Speak tenderly to Jerusalem, and proclaim to her
that her service is at an end,
her guilt is expiated;
Indeed, she has received from the hand of the LORD
double for all her sins.
A voice cries out:
In the desert prepare a way for the LORD!
Make straight in the wasteland
a highway for our God!
Every valley shall be filled in,
every mountain and hill shall be made low;
The rugged land shall be made a plain,
the rough country, a broad valley.
Then the glory of the Lord shall be revealed,
and all mankind shall see it together;
for the mouth of the LORD has spoken.

ISAIAH 40:1–5

PRAYER

Author of life, comfort me on those days when everything else fails to comfort. Protect me from the author of sin whose whispers tease and taunt, tempting me to look elsewhere for my purpose and true happiness. Speak tenderly to me in your still, small voice, reminding me that my satisfaction lies in you alone and can never be found outside the glory of your divine friendship.

ADVENT ACTION

How can you be better prepared to receive the Lord in a more profound way this liturgical season? Is there practical clutter or emotional confusion in your life that you need to clear up? Take the opportunity on this Advent day to accomplish one preparatory task that will free up some time for a deeper spiritual focus as you approach Christmas.

DAY 14

$\mathcal{G}$od wills that we keep His commandments, because when we desire a particular thing, we do not only will what we desire, but we also will whatever enables us to obtain it. Thus, a physician, in order to restore a man to health, also wills his diet, his medicine, and so on. Now God wills us to obtain eternal life: "If thou wouldst enter life, keep the commandments."

God's will is good....well-pleasing, and though displeasing to others, yet delightful to those who love His will....God's will is perfect: "Be ye perfect as your heavenly Father is perfect."

So when we say, *Thy will be done....*

...[W]e must observe here that we have something to learn from the very manner of expression. For He does not say *Do* or *Let us do* but *Thy will be done.* This is because two things are required in order to obtain eternal life: the grace of God and man's will. And although God made man without man's help, He does not sanctify him without his cooperation. As Augustine says, "He Who created thee without thyself, will not justify thee without thyself," because He wishes man to cooperate: "Turn ye unto me and I will turn unto you." "By the grace of God I am what I am, and His grace in me hath not been void." Presume not therefore on yourself, but trust in the grace of God; nor be neglectful, but do your upmost.

THE THREE GREATEST PRAYERS

Mary said, "Behold, I am the handmaid of the Lord. May it be done to me according to your word." Then the angel departed from her.

Blessed are you who believed that what was spoken to you by the Lord would be fulfilled.

And Mary said:

"My soul proclaims the greatness of the Lord;
my spirit rejoices in God my savior.

For he has looked upon his handmaid's lowliness;
behold, from now on will all ages call me blessed.

The Mighty One has done great things for me,
and holy is his name."

LUKE 1:38, 45–49

PRAYER

Divine physician, you came into the world to restore me to full health, but you seek my cooperation in that healing. Help me this Advent to open myself like Mary to trust my Father's will. Help me especially to allow divine healing to enter the painful places in my life. Let me live again the freedom and harmony of God's commandments. Give me the courage to accept that I am what I am by God's grace. I am his work in progress, one in which his will, with my trusting cooperation, is always being done in me.

ADVENT ACTION

When do you experience fragmentation, alienation, division in your life? At home? At work? Where do you spread division, intentionally or unintentionally? Reflect openly and honestly with a trusted family member or friend today about what you need to be freer *from* in order to be freer *for* God's will at home, at work, or wherever the day finds you.

DAY 15

The first thing a Christian needs is faith, without which no man is a faithful Christian. Faith confers four benefits:

Faith unites the soul to God, because by faith the Christian soul is in a sense wedded to God: "I will espouse thee to myself in faith." For this reason, when we are baptized, we begin by confessing our faith when we are asked, "Do you believe in God?" For Baptism is the first of the Sacraments of faith....

Faith introduces eternal life into us, for eternal life is nothing else than to know God....This knowledge of God begins in us by faith, and is perfected in the life to come, when we shall know Him as He is: "Faith is the substance of things to be hoped for." So no man can obtain the happiness of heaven, which is the true knowledge of God, unless he knows Him first by faith....

Faith is our guide in the present life, since in order to lead a good life a man needs to know what is necessary to live rightly.... "The just shall live in his faith."

This is also shown from the fact that before the coming of Christ none of the philosophers was able, however great his effort, to know as much about God or about the means necessary for obtaining eternal life, as any old woman knows by faith since Christ came down upon earth.

THE THREE GREATEST PRAYERS

Hear my voice Lord, when I call;
    have mercy on me and answer me.
"Come," says my heart, "seek God's face";
    your face, LORD, do I seek!
Do not hide your face from me;
    do not repel your servant in anger.
You are my help; do not cast me off;
    do not forsake me, God my savior!
Even if my father and mother forsake me,
    the LORD will take me in.
LORD, show me your way;
    lead me on a level path
    because of my enemies.
Do not abandon me to the will of my foes;
    malicious and lying witnesses have risen against me.
But I believe I shall enjoy the LORD's goodness
    in the land of the living.
Wait for the LORD, take courage;
    be stouthearted, wait for the LORD!

PSALM 27:7–14

PRAYER

God my Savior, waiting is the birthplace of faith. Give me the privilege of being the nursemaid at the birth of faith in another by being a witness of confident waiting. In all things, may I seek your face and not be consumed with my own. In all things, may I find the courage to wait in faithful expectation for my soul to be united with yours.

ADVENT ACTION

Faith does not grow in a vacuum, but through the exercise of trust. One suggested exercise: pray the Apostles' Creed slowly and thoughtfully, mindful of each article of belief that makes up our Catholic faith.

DAY 16

It was unheard of that an angel should show reverence to a human being, until one of them greeted the Blessed Virgin reverently, saying, *Hail.* In ancient times, reverence was shown by men to angels, but not by angels to men, because angels are greater than man....

...until one should be found in human nature who would surpass the angels in three ways—such was the Blessed Virgin....

Accordingly, the Blessed Virgin surpasses the angels...in her fullness of grace...as regards her soul, in which dwelt a plenitude of grace. For God's grace is given for two purposes: the performance of good deeds and the avoidance of evil....after Christ she was free from sin more than any other saint....

...[T]he Blessed Virgin was conceived but not born in original sin....

...[and] is an example of all virtues.

...[T]he soul of the Blessed Virgin was so full of grace that it overflowed into her flesh, fitting it for the conception of God's Son. Thus Hugh of St. Victor says, "The Holy Ghost had so kindled in her heart the fire of divine love that it worked wonders in her flesh, yea, even so that she gave birth to God made man." And St. Luke says: "For the Holy One that shall be born of thee shall be called the Son of God."

THE THREE GREATEST PRAYERS

…"Hail, favored one! The Lord is with you." But she was greatly troubled at what was said and pondered what sort of greeting this might be. Then the angel said to her, "Do not be afraid, Mary, for you have found favor with God. Behold you will conceive in your womb and bear a son, and you shall name him Jesus. But Mary said to the angel, "How can this be, since I have no relations with a man?" And the angel said to her in reply, "The Holy Spirit will come upon you, and the power of the Most High will overshadow you. Therefore the child to be born will be called holy, the Son of God. And behold, Elizabeth, your relative, has also conceived a son in her old age, and this is the sixth month for her who was called barren; for nothing will be impossible for God.

LUKE 1:28–31, 34–37

PRAYER

Hail Mary, favored one, help me to not be afraid. But if I am, help me then to go forward in the face of my fears as you did. Intercede for me, that my soul might be filled with the grace of God's presence in this season of holy anticipation. On my behalf, ask God to enkindle in my heart that same fire of divine love that so radiated from yours, that I might work wonders for his glory as you did.

ADVENT ACTION

If you are to be more fully open to receiving God's grace in this season of preparation, you need to deal honestly with your fears. Today, make a list of what you are most afraid of and share it with someone you trust—a spouse, close friend, son, or daughter.

DAY 17

*O*nly the Virgin's Fruit affords that which Eve sought in her fruit....

...In her fruit, Eve sought to become like gods, knowing good and evil (which the devil falsely promised)....For through eating the fruit, Eve did not become like God, but *un*like Him, since by sinning she turned away from God, her salvation, and was expelled from paradise. On the other hand, the Blessed Virgin found likeness to God in the Fruit of her womb—and so do all followers of Christ—since through Christ we are united and likened to God. "When He shall appear, we shall be like unto Him, for we shall see Him as he is."

...Eve in her fruit sought pleasure, since it was good to eat; yet she did not find it, for at once she perceived that she was naked, and tasted sorrow. But in the Fruit of the Blessed Virgin we find sweetness and salvation. "He that eateth my flesh...hath eternal life."

...Eve in her fruit sought beauty: Eve's fruit was fair to the eyes. Yet fairer still is the Virgin's Fruit on Whom the angels long to gaze: "Thou art the fairer than the sons of men." This is because He is the 'brightness of the Father's glory." Accordingly, Eve could not find in her fruit that which no sinner can find in his sin....

Thus is the Virgin blessed, but still more blessed is her Fruit.

THE THREE GREATEST PRAYERS

When Elizabeth heard Mary's greeting, the infant leaped in her womb, and Elizabeth, filled with the Holy Spirit, cried out in a loud voice and said, "Most blessed are you among women, and blessed is the fruit for your womb. And how does this happen to me, that the mother of my Lord should come to me? For at the moment the sound of your greeting reached my ears, the infant in my womb leaped for joy."

LUKE 1:41–44

PRAYER

Brightness of the Father's glory, shine a light on those places in my heart that are most unlike my God and Creator. Then give me the desire and fortitude to change those things with your help. For it is through you that I am united and likened to the Father.

ADVENT ACTION

What should you let go of in your daily habits, actions, or conversations? Each of us knows those nagging areas in our lives that need addressing, but to paraphrase Augustine, we say: "Ah, yes, Lord, but not just yet!" Set aside at least ten minutes today to be completely honest in talking to the Lord about what he is challenging you to face.

DAY 18

*T*herefore God's incarnation…was necessary for the restoration of human nature…

Let us consider this, beginning with man's furtherance in good.

First, with regard to faith, greater assurance is guaranteed when the belief rests on God himself speaking. Thus Augustine writes, *Truth itself, the Son of God made man, established and confirmed faith that men more confidently might journey to it.*

Second, as to hope, which is lifted to the heights, for, to quote Augustine, *nothing is so needful to build up our hope than for us to be shown how much God loves us. And what is a better sign of this than the Son of God deigning to share our nature?*

Third, as to charity, which is most greatly enkindled by the Incarnation for, as Augustine asks, *what greater cause is there for the coming of the Lord than to show God's love for us?* He goes on, *If we have been slow to love, let us not be slow to love in return.*

SUMMA THEOLOGIAE

No, in all these things we conquer overwhelmingly through him who loved us. For I am convinced that neither death, nor life, nor angels, nor principalities, nor present things, nor future things, nor powers, nor height, nor depth, nor any other creature will be able to separate us from the love God in Christ Jesus our Lord.

ROMANS 8:37–39

And again Isaiah says: "The root of Jesse shall come, raised up to rule the Gentiles; in him shall the Gentiles hope. May the God of hope fill you with all joy and peace in believing, so that you may abound in hope by the power of the Holy Spirit."

ROMANS 15:13

PRAYER

Generous Father, through grace, each day you send me out with the tools of faith, hope, and love to build your kingdom. But sometimes I leave the tools in the toolbox on a shelf at home. Be patient with me when, distracted, I am slow to love you—and to love you in my brother and sister. Refuel my faith and heighten my hope that charity might once again be reborn in my heart.

ADVENT ACTION

In the business of life, it is easy to put God on a shelf and leave the three theological virtues of faith, hope, and love hanging in the closet. Take God with you into your day by emailing someone in doubt to strengthen their faith or by offering encouragement and a word of hope to someone who is struggling. Make a conscious gesture toward someone who has ongoing difficulties with low self-esteem.

✦✦✦ DAY 19 ✦✦✦✦✦✦✦✦✦✦✦✦✦✦✦✦✦

Since the work of the Incarnation was directed chiefly to the restoration of the human race through the removal of sin, it is clear that it was not fitting that God become incarnate from the beginning of the human race before sin; medicine is given only to the sick. Therefore, as the Lord himself teaches, *It is not the healthy who need a physician, but they who are sick. For I am not come to call the just, but sinners.*

...Love does not delay to aid a friend, yet with a care for the right timing and for personal conditions. If a doctor were to give medicine to one who is ill at the very beginning of the sickness, it would be of less value, or even could do more harm than good. So also the Lord does not immediately provide the Incarnation to the human race as a remedy, lest it be spurned out of pride, before men recognized their own weakness.

SUMMA THEOLOGIAE

Since everything is to be dissolved in this way, what sort of persons ought [you] to be, conducting yourselves in holiness and devotion, waiting for and hastening the coming of the day of God, because of which the heavens will be dissolved in flames and the elements melted by fire. But according to his promise we await new heavens and a new earth in which righteousness dwells.

Therefore, beloved, since you await these things, be eager to be found without spot or blemish before him, at peace. And consider the patience of our Lord as salvation…

2 PETER 3:11–15

PRAYER

Intimate friend, you are there for me at the time and place I need you the most. Your peace is medicine for my soul. You don't take away or enable my weakness, but like a true friend, you supply the strength for me to transcend it. Help me to patiently await your timetable in all things and not be anxious about my own. In my eagerness to receive all the aid that you have to give me, guide my conduct so that it leaves little doubt of the peaceful trust I place in you.

ADVENT ACTION

Our Lord says: "I leave you peace, my peace I give you." He sends us out like paramedics to offer his medicine of peace to the sick in soul. Decide today to visit a friend, in person or by phone, who is spiritually ill; ask the Lord to let you be his instrument of incarnate healing.

DAY 20

God wills three things in our regard, which we pray to be fulfilled….God wills that we may have eternal life, because whoever makes a certain thing for a certain purpose wills that purpose for it….

When a thing attains the end for which it was made it is said to be saved, whereas when it fails to reach that end it is said to be lost. Now God made man for eternal life; and consequently, when man obtains eternal life he is saved, which is God's will: "This is the will of my Father Who sent me, that whosoever beholdeth the Son and believeth in Him, have eternal life." This will is already fulfilled in the angels and saints, who are in heaven, who see, know, and enjoy God.

THE THREE GREATEST PRAYERS

Then the angel showed me the river of life-giving water, sparkling like crystal, flowing from the throne of God and of the Lamb down the middle of the street....Nothing accursed will be found there anymore. The throne of God and of the Lamb will be in it, and his servants will worship him. They will look upon his face and his name will be on their foreheads. Night will be no more, nor will they need light from lamp or sun, for the Lord God shall give them light, and they shall reign forever and ever.

"Behold, I am coming soon....

"I, Jesus, sent my angel to give you this testimony for the churches. I am the root and offspring of David, the bright morning star."

Let the one who thirsts come forward and the one who wants it receive the gift of life-giving water.

The one who gives this testimony says, "Yes, I am coming soon." Amen! Come, Lord Jesus!

REVELATION 22:1–2A, 3–5, 7, 16, 17B, 20

PRAYER

Offspring of David, Bright Morning Star, you came that we might know the purpose we have here on earth: to be with you in eternal glory. You give yourself wholly and completely to us for an eternity. But Lord, our eternal life does not begin after our physical death, but now in the intimate friendship you hold out to us this day, in this moment, among these circumstances of our lives, among these people who make up our daily lives.

ADVENT ACTION

Do you begin each task with the end in mind? Do you make choices based on the purpose for which God has destined you? Today, review how the Lord's purpose for your life impacts your decision-making.

DAY 21

*G*od incarnation was necessary for human salvation....

Fourth, as to right living, we are set an example. Augustine says, in a Christmas sermon, *Not man, who can be seen, should be followed, but God, who cannot be seen. So then, that we might be shown one who would be both seen and followed, God became man.*

Fifth, as to the full sharing in divinity, which is true happiness and the purpose of human life. This comes to us through the humanity of Christ, for, in Augustine's phrase, *God was made man that man might become God.*

Summa Theologiae

When I see your heavens, the work of your fingers,
    the moon and the stars you set in place—
What are humans that you are mindful of them,
    mere mortals that you care for them?
Yet you have made them little less than a god,
    crowned them with glory and honor.
You have given them rule over the works of your hands,
    put all things at their feet:
All sheep and oxen,
    even the beasts of the field,
The birds of the air, the fish of the sea,
    and whatever swims the path of the seas.
O LORD, our Lord,
    how awesome is your name through the earth!

PSALM 8:4–10

PRAYER

God of power and might, it seems incomprehensible that you call "little me" to share in mighty you. But you do, endowing me with an unfathomable dignity, unique and unprecedented in all of creation. Remind me of that noble dignity. May I wear it not as a badge of personal honor, but as a mantle of faithful gratitude that witnesses to my purpose as a human being and to your glory as the God who stoops down to a frail humanity and lifts me up… again and again.

ADVENT ACTION

When was the last time you really thought about the purpose of your life, your true happiness? Is it found in sharing God's life each day or in superficial conversations or activities? Take a brief mental or written inventory today of those whose example you tend to follow. What is your "default" image (like the screen to which your computer automatically defaults) of true happiness and purpose in life?

DAY 22

*H*uman nature is raised by the incarnation to its highest perfection, and so it was not fitting that the Incarnation take place from the beginning of the human race. Nevertheless, the incarnate Word is the efficient cause of human fulfillment, according to *John, Of his fullness we have all received;* accordingly the Incarnation ought not to be delayed until the end of the world. Yet the achievement of glory, to which human nature is finally brought by the incarnate Word, will come at the end of the world.

A second reason is the effect, human salvation. The following text is pertinent, *It is in the power of the giver to show mercy when and to the extent that he chooses. He came, indeed, when he knew that aid should be given and that his gift would be welcome. When, therefore, by a kind of illness of the human race, man's knowledge of him became dim and morals weakened, God deigned to choose Abraham in whom there would be a model of renewed knowledge and conduct. And when reverence again weakened, he gave the written Law through Moses. Still the Gentiles despised it and would not subject themselves to it...but the Lord, moved by mercy, sent his Son who, after giving to all the remission of their sins, might offer those made righteous to God the Father.* But if this remedy had been postponed until the end of the world, knowledge of God and reverence and moral decency would have been totally removed from the earth.

SUMMA THEOLOGIAE

In him we have redemption by his blood, the forgiveness of transgressions, in accord with the riches of his grace that he lavished upon us. In all wisdom and insight, he made it known to us the mystery of his will in accord with his favor that he set forth in him as a plan for the fullness of times, to sum up all things in Christ, in heaven and on earth.

In him, we were also chosen, destined in accord with the purpose of the One who accomplishes all things according to the intention of his will, so that we might exist for the praise of his glory, we who first hoped in Christ.

EPHESIANS 1:7–12

PRAYER

All-knowing Father, your compassion has known no bounds, even when man turned a deaf ear to Abraham, Moses, and the prophets. Moved by mercy, you sent your own Son when you knew he was needed most. Help me to know those days when I especially need my Savior. When you send him through human voices, may the light of my faith not be found dim, but instead shining brightly, giving praise to your glory and ready to receive the awaited gift.

ADVENT ACTION

We exist for the praise of God's glory. How do you get in touch with that glory on a day-to-day basis? Take a walk outside today if possible, or take a few moments to gaze through your window. Note and relish the riches of God's grace lavished upon us in nature. However you can, feel for a moment the sun's rays and know God's warmth; feel the wind on your cheek and know God's caress.

DAY 23

*T*he Son's becoming incarnate was altogether appropriate.
And first from the meaning of the union. Like is fittingly
joined to like. We can look to one sort of general affinity between
the Son, the Word of God, and all creatures: the craftsman's
mental word, i.e. his idea, is a pattern for whatever he fashions;
so too the Word, God's eternal conception, is the exemplar for
all creation. Creatures are first established, though changeably,
in their proper kinds by a sharing in that likeness; similarly, it is
fitting that creatures be restored to their eternal and changeless
perfection through the Word being united, not participatively,
but in person with the creature. The craftsman repairs his own
work when it has been damaged on the same mental model he
used in making it. A special affinity exists, however, in a further way between the Word and human nature from the fact
that the Word is the intelligible expression of divine wisdom,
and as such is the source of all human wisdom. Man therefore
reaches his perfection in wisdom…through a participation in

the Word of God, even as the pupil makes progress by receiving the teacher's word.

Summa Theologiae

...that the God of our Lord Jesus Christ, the Father of glory, may give you a spirit of wisdom and revelation resulting in knowledge of him. May the eyes of [your] hearts be enlightened, that you may know what is the hope that belongs to his call, what are the riches of glory in his inheritance among the holy ones and what is the surpassing greatness of his power for us who believe in accord with the exercise of his great might....

Ephesians 1:17–19

Prayer

Wise and holy Father, all of life is but a classroom for the learning of your wisdom. Make me a good and faithful pupil, quick to receive your instructions, eager to put what I learn into practice, and grateful always to the divine craftsman who fashions the pattern of his life in me... from his very idea of me.

Advent Action

What do you most need to learn from God in this holy season? It will take courage and trust, but today ask this question of two people who know you well.

DAY 24

A gift is so named from its being given.…[R]eflect that a gift, according to Aristotle, is literally a giving that can have no return, i.e. it is not given with repayment in mind and as such denotes a giving out of good will. Now the basis for such gracious giving is love; the reason we give something to another spontaneously is that we will good to him. And so what we give first to anyone is the love itself with which we love him. Clearly, then, love has the quality of being our first gift; through love we give all other loving gifts. Since, then, as shown, the Holy Spirit comes forth as Love, he proceeds as being the first Gift. So Augustine teaches that *through the Gift who is the Holy Spirit, the many individual gifts are distributed to Christ's members.*

SUMMA THEOLOGIAE

I give thanks to my God always on your account for the grace of God bestowed on you in Christ Jesus, that in him you were enriched in every way, with all discourse and all knowledge, as testimony to Christ was confirmed among you, so that you are not lacking in any spiritual gift as you wait for the revelation of our Lord Jesus Christ. He will keep you firm until the end, irreproachable on the day of our Lord Jesus [Christ]. God is faithful, and by him you were called to fellowship with his Son, Jesus Christ our Lord.

1 CORINTHIANS 1:4–9

PRAYER

Holy Spirit, you are God's gift to me. Through you I receive gifts of courage, charity, patience, and self-control. Through you I know the love between the Father and the Son he sent, a love I am invited to join. But I so often doubt my gifts. Wherever I find myself today, enrich me with the knowledge of my own spiritual gifts and the firm resolve to use them for the building up of God's kingdom.

ADVENT ACTION

Are you aware of your gifts? If so, who do you use them for, yourself or God? If not, what are you going to do to find out what they are? We always remember the negative things people say about us. Today, listen for the positive comments and give thanks to God for the revelation of a gift you can use for him.

*T*he Lord is said to hear the desire of the poor either because desire is the cause of their petition, since a petition is an expression of desire, or to show how quickly the poor are heard, for God hears the poor even before they offer a prayer....

...Prayer motivated by charity tends toward God in two ways: first, in so far as the thing requested is concerned, because when we pray we should ask principally to be united to God....

...[S]econdly, in so far as the one praying is concerned, because one ought to approach the person from whom he requests something, either in place when from a man, or in mind when from God. Hence Dionysius says, *when we call upon God in our prayers we unveil our mind in his presence....*

...We must pray, not in order to inform God of our needs and desires, but in order to remind ourselves that in these matters we need divine assistance.... [O]ur motive in praying is not that we may change the divine decree, but that we might obtain that which God has decreed will be obtained by prayer. Even without asking, God bestows many things on us out of liberality.

Yet for our own good he wishes to give us certain things upon our request....

...Through prayer man offers reverence to God because he subjects himself to God and professes that God is the source of all that he is and all that he has....

Rejoice in the Lord always. I say it again: rejoice! Your kindness should be known to all. The Lord is near. Have no anxiety at all, but in everything, by prayer and petition, with thanksgiving, make your requests known to God. Then the peace of God that surpasses all understanding will guard your hearts and minds in Christ Jesus.

PHILIPPIANS 4:4–7

PRAYER

God of all that I am and all that I have, sometimes I just can't seem to pray. Why do I worry so much? Why am I so anxious? In you, every desire is fulfilled and my deepest needs are met. Help me, in those moments when I am feeling the most impoverished spiritually or emotionally, to know that even the desire to pray is itself a prayer to you. May each attempt begin and end with a silent "Thank you."

ADVENT ACTION

This week, schedule some time for centering prayer. Just like it sounds, use a prayerful word or phrase to center yourself in God's presence for about five to seven minutes. After you have done this a few times, you might work up to ten or fifteen minutes. Pick a quiet place. In a relaxed but alert posture, say the prayer word in your mind, for example, "Jesus," "Abba-Father," "Spirit," "peace," or "joy." You may instead use a phrase like "Be still and know that I am God," or "In you I live and move and have my being." When you feel centered in God's loving presence, let it go. Calmly return to it when distractions disturb you. Then slowly let it go again. Finally, end with an Our Father, praying very slowly and thoughtfully.

DAY 26

The Lord's Prayer is the best of all [prayers] because as Augustine says, *If we pray rightly and fittingly, we can say nothing else but what is contained in the Lord's Prayer.* Prayer, as it were, places our desires before God, so asking for something in prayer is right provided it is right to desire it. In the Lord's Prayer we not only ask for all the things we can rightly desire, but also in the sequence that we ought to desire them, so that this prayer not only teaches us to ask things, but also in what order we ought to desire them.

…Our goal is God, in whom our desires tend in two ways, first by willing the glory of God, and secondly by willing to enjoy his glory.…

Prayer is not offered to God in order to change his mind, but in order to excite confidence in us. Such confidence is fostered principally by considering God's charity toward us whereby he wills our good: hence we say, "Our Father," and to indicate his excellence powerful to fulfill his charity, "Who art in heaven."

SUMMA THEOLOGIAE

"In praying, do not babble like the pagans, who think that they will be heard because of there many words. Do not be like them. Your Father knows what you need before you ask him.

"This is how you are to pray:
Our Father in heaven,
*   hallowed be your name,*
*   your kingdom come,*
*   your will be done*
*   on earth as in heaven.*
*   Give us today our daily bread;*
and forgive us our debts,
*   as we forgive our debtors;*
and do not subject us to the final test,
*   but deliver us from the evil one."*

MATTHEW 6:7–13

PRAYER

Loving Lord, in your prayer, you taught me not to be afraid to approach my heavenly Father with both the things I need and the things I need to avoid. Help me to not shy away from going to Abba-Father as you always did and confidently expecting his help and listening, for he wills my good. Remind me that I don't need a lot of words, just a lot of love. For your Abba and my Abba ("Daddy") are one and the same.

ADVENT ACTION

Take at least ten minutes today to prayerfully meditate on each line of the Lord's Prayer, relishing the beauty of its simplicity and clarity regarding how we are to pray. Take away a phrase from your reflection to accompany you throughout your day and to keep you close to your heavenly Father's heart.

DAY 27

We use words when speaking to God for one reason and when speaking to men for another. When speaking to another man, we use words in order to express our inward thoughts which the other is unable to know unless they are expressed in words. We praise a man vocally, therefore, so that he or others might know the good opinion we have of him, so that he will be encouraged to do better, and so that others who hear him praised will think well of him, reverence him, and imitate him.

On the other hand, we use words when speaking to God, not in order to manifest our thoughts to him who is the searcher of hearts, but that we may bring ourselves and our listeners to reverence him. Vocal praise of God is necessary, therefore, not for his sake but for our own, since by praising him our devotion is aroused....through praise of God man's affections ascend to God and thus are withdrawn from interests contrary to God....

Vocal praise is useless if it does not come from the heart.... Vocal praise, however, arouses the interior affection of the one praising and prompts others to praise God....We praise God, not for his benefit, but for ours....

SUMMA THEOLOGIAE

Seek the LORD while he may be found,
call him while he is near.
As high as the heavens are above the earth,
so high are my ways above your ways
and my thoughts above your thoughts.
For just as from the heavens
the rain and snow come down
And do not return there
till they have watered the earth,
making it fertile and fruitful,
Giving seed to him who sows
and bread to him who eats,
So shall my word be
that goes forth from my mouth;
It shall not return to me void,
but shall do my will,
achieving the end for which it was sent.

ISAIAH 55:6, 9–11

PRAYER

Searcher of hearts, you know me through and through. You know the word I will speak even before it is on my tongue. May that word I speak be one of praise and gratitude for all you have given me. May it be a word that arouses love and reverence for you in others. Lord, stop my words when they harm rather than help, tear down rather than build up, or risk turning someone away rather than toward you. Let me call on your Holy Spirit to help me know what to say and when to say it, when to speak and when to remain silent.

ADVENT ACTION

Words can either create or destroy. Words can kill. Today, observe closely your conversations and the words you use. At the end of the day, examine your conscience and note the impact of your words on the people and events of your day.

DAY 28

$\mathscr{D}$evotion is an act of the will by which a man promptly gives himself to the service of God....A man forms this idea in one of two ways. The first way is by considering the divine goodness and kindness....Considerations of this type awaken love which is the proximate cause of devotion. The second way is by considering man's weaknesses, which leads to the realization that man must depend upon God....Consideration of things which increase our love for God causes devotion; consideration of things which distract the mind from God impedes devotion.

...The direct and principal effect of devotion is spiritual joy....Considering God's goodness is the principal cause because this is the goal of a man who submits himself to God....Secondarily, devotion is caused by considering our own weaknesses, for this consideration is the starting point from which a devout man proceeds when he trusts not in himself, but instead subjects himself to God....joy is caused because we hope for divine assistance in overcoming our weaknesses.

SUMMA THEOLOGIAE

Awake, awake!
    Put on your strength, O Zion;
Put on your glorious garments,
    O Jerusalem, holy city.
No longer shall the uncircumcised
    or the unclean enter you.
Shake off the dust,
    ascend to the throne, Jerusalem;
Loose the bonds from your neck,
    O captive daughter of Zion!
Hark! Your watchmen raise a cry,
    together they shout for joy,
For they see directly before their eyes,
    the Lord restoring Zion.
The Lord has bared his holy arm
    in the sight of all the nations;
All the ends of the earth will behold
    the salvation of our God.

ISAIAH 52:1–2, 8, 10

PRAYER

God of infinite goodness and compassion, awaken that love in me that fires up faith and fuels its unwavering zeal. In the face of distraction, let me firmly turn my mind and heart back to you. In facing my weaknesses, let me see the road to your divine assistance in overcoming them. For you ask me not if I am worthy, but if I am willing. In willingness, not worthiness, is my spiritual joy discovered.

ADVENT ACTION

Advent is a time to wake up to the deeper meaning behind life's events and encounters. If you are to be prepared to receive God when he shows himself, what act of the will do you have in place? Devotion is an exercise of the soul to awaken love. What daily spiritual exercise can you commit yourself to this Advent? Perhaps it is spiritual reading, praying the rosary, attending Mass, or learning about the life of a saint each day.

PART II

~~~~~

READINGS
FOR THE
CHRISTMAS
SEASON

DAY 1

*A*mong those to whom we are bound to do good are those in some way united to us. Thus, "if any man have not care of his own and especially of those of his house, he hath denied the faith." Now amongst all of our relatives there is none closer than our father and mother. "We ought to love God first," says St. Ambrose, "then our father and mother." Hence, God has given us the Commandment: *Honor thy father and they mother.*"

The Philosopher also gives another reason for this honor to parents, in that we cannot make an equal return to our parents for the great benefits they have granted us....

Parents, indeed, provide three benefits to children:

The first is that they bring us into being....Second, they furnish us nourishment and the support necessary for life.... Instruction is the third benefit that parents provide children....

GOD'S GREATEST GIFTS

Now this is how the birth of Jesus Christ came about. When his mother was betrothed to Joseph, but before they lived together, she was found with child through the Holy Spirit. Joseph her husband, since he was a righteous man, yet unwilling to expose her to shame, decided to divorce her quietly. Such was his intention when behold, the angel of the Lord appeared to him in a dream and said, "Joseph, son of David, do not be afraid to take Mary your wife into your home. For it is through the Holy Spirit that this child is conceived in her. She will have a son and you are to name him Jesus, because he will save his people from their sins." All this took place to fulfill what the Lord had said through the prophet:

"Behold, the virgin shall be with child and bear a son, and they shall name him Emmanuel," which means "God with us."

MATTHEW 1:18–23

PRAYER

All-knowing God, you knew the genteel spirit and generosity of faith that would be needed to raise the special child born in Bethlehem. You chose Mary and Joseph as his parents whose humble "yes" we still honor and revere today. Their consent mirrors the call of all parents to echo the same trust in bringing your sons and daughters into the world and raising them each to be another image of Emmanuel ("God with us"). Remind me to revere the privilege of parenthood and to honor my own parents and family members.

CHRISTMAS ACTION

When is the last time you did something unexpected for your parents or an older relative who nourished your faith and growth as a human being? As Jesus honored his parents, reach out to a member of your family who formed you in faith and who deserves your gratitude and respect. Take a moment this week and write a meaningful note to a parent, relative, or sibling who supported you in your faith and human journey to who you are today.

DAY 2

[By the Incarnation] **our faith is strengthened**. For instance, if anyone were to tell us about a distant country which he had never visited, we would not believe him to the same extent as if he had been there. Accordingly, before Christ came into the world, the patriarchs, prophets, and John the Baptist said certain things about God, but men did not believe them as they believe Christ Who was with God, Who indeed was one with God. For this reason our faith is very strong, seeing that we have received it from Christ....So it is that many mysteries of faith have been made known to us after the coming of Christ, which until then were hidden.

Our hope is raised, because it is evident that God's Son took our flesh and came to us not for a trifling reason, but for our exceedingly great good. He bound Himself to us, as it were, by deigning to take a human soul and body and to be born of a Virgin, in order to bestow His Godhead on us. Thus, He became man that man might become God....

Our charity is inflamed, because there is no greater proof of God's love than that God the Creator became a creature, that our Lord became our brother, and that the Son of God became the Son of man: "God so loved the world that he gave His only begotten son." The very thought of this should kindle and inflame our hearts with the love of God.

THE THREE GREATEST PRAYERS

The angel of the Lord appeared before them and the glory of the Lord shone around them, and they were struck with great fear. The angel said to them: "Do not be afraid; for behold, I proclaim to you good news of great joy that will be for all the people. For today in the city of David a savior has been born for you who is Messiah and Lord. And this will be a sign for you; you will find him wrapped in swaddling clothes and lying in a manger."

LUKE 2:9–12

PRAYER

Loving Father, of all the ambassadors you sent, the patriarchs, the prophets, John the Baptist, and others, none was more revealing of the depth of your love than your own Son. His entrance into human history fuels my faith, harnesses my hope, and links my love with all who bear the name "Christian." As he became human, may I allow him to make me divine.

CHRISTMAS ACTION

Faith, hope, and charity are spiritual muscles. To grow, they must be exercised, just as the physical muscles of the body have to be exercised. This week I will exercise *faith* by reading a passage from Scripture, *hope* by sitting in silent meditation of the Word of God, and *charity* by acting on the Word though a concrete action on behalf of another.

DAY 3

*T*hrough this "spirit of adoption" that we receive, we cry: "*Abba* (Father)," as is said in Romans 8:15. Hence our Lord began His prayer by calling upon the Father, saying, "Father," to teach us that our prayer must be based on this hope. By uttering the name, "Father," man's affection is prepared to pray with a pure disposition, and also to obtain what he hopes for. Moreover, sons ought to be imitators of their parents. Therefore, he who professes that God is his Father ought to try to be an imitator of God, by avoiding things that make him unlike God and by earnestly praying for those perfections that make him like to God. Hence we are commanded in Jeremiah 3:19: "Thou shalt call me *Father* and shalt not cease to walk after me."

LIGHT OF FAITH: THE COMPENDIUM OF THEOLOGY

For in hope we were saved. Now hope that sees for itself is not hope. But if we hope for what we do not see, we wait with endurance.

In the same way, the Spirit too comes to the aid of our weakness; for we do not know how to pray as we ought, but the Spirit itself intercedes with inexpressible groanings. And the one who searches hearts knows what is the intention of the Spirit, because it intercedes for the holy ones according to God's will.

ROMANS 8:24–27

PRAYER

Lord, you teach me to reach out to God with affection, not fear, as to a loving parent. By your example, you taught me again and again to cry out with confident hope, "Abba, Father." When I come to you in prayer each day, you will teach me if I truly listen, to give myself over courageously to the Spirit that prays within me when I no longer can or know how.

CHRISTMAS ACTION

If Christmas is the celebration of the new life born in you by Christ's coming, where does the evidence of that new man or woman in Christ manifest itself? Are you an "imitator" of God? Who do you model yourself after in the workplace? At home? In the neighborhood? Pause for five minutes before your day begins and just before it ends to reflect on who you wanted to "walk after" throughout the day and who you actually *did* walk after.

DAY 4

$\mathcal{J}$t is most fitting to manifest the unseen things of God
through things that are not seen, for this is the purpose of
the whole world, as the Apostle teaches, *The invisible things of God
are there for the mind to see in the things that he has made.* But,
as Damascene remarks, through the mystery of the Incarnation
*the goodness, wisdom, justice, and power or strength of God are
shown: goodness, for he did not disdain the weakness of his own
handiwork; justice, because he vanquished the tyrant by none other
than man and yet did not snatch man away by violence; wisdom,
for he found the most apt payment for a most exacting debt; power
or strength that is infinite, for what could be greater than for God
to become man?*

SUMMA THEOLOGIAE

I am the Lord and there is no other,
*   there is no God besides me.*
It is I that arm you, though you know me not,
*   so that toward the rising and the setting of the sun*
*   men may know that there is none besides me.*
I am the Lord and there is no other;
*   I form the light, and create the darkness,*
I make well-being and create woe;
*   I, the Lord, do all these things.*
Let justice descend, O heaven, like dew from above,
*   like a gentle rain let the skies drop it down.*
Let the earth open and salvation bud forth;
*   let justice also spring up!*
*   I the Lord have created this.*

ISAIAH 45:5–8

PRAYER

Creator God, I am your handiwork. You made me to be a good, wise, and just instrument of your power. Strengthen my resolve to be what you have destined me to be, what you show me I *can* be through Jesus, the Christ, your face of justice in the world.

CHRISTMAS ACTION

When you take a moment to examine your conscience today, where are you most lacking in basic goodness, justice, wisdom, and spiritual power? Throughout this day, reflect upon your patterns of conversation and action and see how God's goodness, justice, wisdom, and the power of God are transparent in your example.

DAY 5

𝒯o restore man, who had been laid low by sin, to the heights of divine glory, the Word of the eternal Father, though containing all things within His immensity, willed to become small. This he did, not by putting aside His greatness, but by taking to Himself our littleness.…Man's salvation consists in knowing the truth, so that the human mind may not be confused by diverse errors; in making for the right goal, so that man may not fall away from true happiness by pursuing wrong ends.…

Knowledge of the truth necessary for man's salvation is comprised within a few brief articles of Faith. The Apostle says in Romans 9:28: "A short word shall the Lord make upon the Earth" and in a later passage he adds: "This is the word of faith, which we preach." In a short prayer Christ clearly marked out man's right course; and in teaching us to say this prayer, He showed us the goal of our striving and hope. In a single precept of charity He summed up that human justice which consists in observing the Law: "Love therefore is the fulfilling of the Law."

LIGHT OF FAITH: THE COMPENDIUM OF THEOLOGY

Have among yourselves the same attitude
    that is also yours in Christ Jesus,
Who, though he was in the form of God,
    did not deem equality with God
    something to be grasped.
Rather, he emptied himself,
    taking the form of a slave,
    coming in human likeness;
    and found human in appearance,
    he humbled himself,
    becoming obedient to death,
    even death on a cross.
Because of this, God greatly exalted him
    and bestowed on him the name
    that is above every name,
    that at the name of Jesus
    every knee should bend,
    of those in heaven and on earth and under the earth,
    and every tongue confess that
    Jesus Christ is Lord,
    to the glory of God the Father.

PHILIPPIANS 2:5–11

PRAYER

Mighty God, you saved me by becoming small that I might know the largeness of your love. You became little that I might grasp the greatness of your truth. You became empty that I might taste the fullness of your joy. Help me to become small, little, and empty that I might embrace more readily your love, your truth, your joy.

CHRISTMAS ACTION

The unfathomable gift of Christmas is that the mighty God stoops down to raise "lowly us" to the dizzying heights of his divine life and love. If the almighty God can stoop down to raise us up, where can you lower your pride and ego today to lift another in need of divine life and love? Let the Spirit lead you to that person.

DAY 6

*I*t should be urged that human well-being called for school-
ing in what God has revealed....

Above all because God destines us for an end beyond the
grasp of reason; according to Isaiah, *Eye hath not seen, O God,
without thee what thou has prepared for them that love thee.*
Now, we have to recognize an end before we can stretch out
and exert ourselves for it. Hence, the necessity for our welfare
that divine truths surpassing reason should be signified to us
through divine revelation.

We also stood in need of being instructed by divine revelation
even in religious matters the human reason is able to investi-
gate....on knowing this depends our whole welfare, which is in
God....Admittedly the reason should not pry into things too
high for human knowledge, nevertheless, when they are revealed
by God they should be welcomed by faith: indeed the passage
in *Ecclesiasticus* goes on, *Many things are shown thee above the
understanding of men.* And on them Christian teaching rests.

SUMMA THEOLOGIAE

In times past, God spoke in partial and various ways to our
ancestors through the prophets; in these last days, he spoke
to us through a son, whom he made heir of all things and
through whom he created the universe,
>*who is the refulgence of his glory,*
>>*the very imprint of his being,*
>*and who sustains all things by his mighty word.*
>*When he had accomplished purification from sins,*
>*he took his seat at the right hand*
>*of the Majesty on high,*
>*as far superior to the angels*
>*as the name he has inherited*
>*is more excellent than theirs.*

HEBREWS 1:1–4

PRAYER

Child of Bethlehem, my faith welcomes you once again. You are the revelation of the Father, the manifestation of his presence in the world, the tangible imprint of his very being among us. Sustain me in my faith as my ancestors were sustained in their faith by reminding me of the end for which I was created. Stretch me beyond the grasp of reason to an abandonment of self that reflects confidence in my Christian teaching to all I encounter. Let my witness be so bold that my life makes no sense save for my belief in God.

CHRISTMAS ACTION

The Incarnate Word of God is a living Word. How do you carry that living Word spoken to your ancestors through his Son into our world today? Consider a volunteer opportunity at your parish, your child's school, or the local food pantry or shelter where your public witness can speak powerfully to others.

*T*he Lord's words, *No longer will I call you servants but my friends*, can be explained only in terms of charity, which, therefore, is friendship.

...[N]ot all love has the character of friendship, but that only which goes with well wishing, namely when we so love another as to will what is good for him. For if what we will is our own good, as when we love wine or a horse or the like, it is a love not of friendship but of desire. It makes no sense to talk of somebody being friends with wine or a horse.

Yet, goodwill alone is not enough for friendship for this requires a mutual loving....But such reciprocal good will is based on something in common.

Now there is a sharing of man with God by his sharing his happiness with us, and it is on this that a friendship is based.... Now the love which is based on this sort of fellowship is charity. Accordingly it is clear that charity is a friendship of man and God.

SUMMA THEOLOGIAE

..."No one can receive anything except what has been given him from heaven. You yourselves can testify that I said [that] I am not the Messiah, but that I was sent before him. He who has the bride is the bridegroom; the best man, who stands and listens for him, rejoices greatly at the bridegroom's voice. So this joy of mine has been made complete. He must increase; I must decrease.*

JOHN 3:27–30

PRAYER

Lord, I ache for your friendship. Help me to daily walk through the door of charity that opens wide to that divine friendship revealed in the coming of Christ. I will need courage, Lord, the courage to let my fears, preoccupations, and my agenda decrease so that the loving voice of your friendship might increase.

CHRISTMAS ACTION

Today, stop three times—once in the morning, once in the afternoon and once in the evening—and ask yourself: Whose voice am I listening to? Is it the Bridegroom's or the television? Whose friendship is influencing me? Is it my intimate friendship with God or the prevailing culture?

$\mathcal{T}$he ultimate end of all things is necessarily the divine goodness....

[S]ince the divine goodness could not be adequately represented by one creature alone, on account of the distance that separates each creature from God, it had to be represented by many creatures, so that what is lacking to one might be supplied by another.

...[T]he multiplicity and distinction existing among things were devised by the divine intellect and were carried out in the real order so that the divine goodness might be mirrored by created things in variety, and that different things might participate in the divine goodness in varying degree. Thus, the very order existing among diverse things issues in a certain beauty, which should call to mind the divine wisdom.

LIGHT OF FAITH: THE COMPENDIUM ON THEOLOGY

For Wisdom is mobile…
>   *and she penetrates and pervades all things*
>   *by reason of her purity.*

For she is an aura of the might of God
>   *and a pure effusion of the glory of the Almighty;*
>   *therefore nought that is sullied enters into her.*

For she is the refulgence of eternal light,
>   *the spotless mirror of the power of God,*
>   *the image of goodness.*

And she, who is one, can do all things,
>   *and renews everything while herself perduring;*

And passing into holy souls from age to age,
>   *she produces friends of God and prophets.*

For there is nought God loves,
>   *be it not one who dwells with Wisdom.*

WISDOM 7:24–28

PRAYER

Wise and loving God, that I may come to know you more deeply and that others may come to know you through me, pervade and penetrate my entire being. Make me a pure emanation of your glory, a radiant reflection of eternal light, a spotless mirror of your presence in the world, an image of your goodness. Lord help me to live with your wisdom and not my own, that I may be a beacon of your friendship for others.

CHRISTMAS ACTION

The wisdom of God's friendship does not come by osmosis, but by habits of prayer and study. The octave of Christmas is often treated as an afterthought, but strive to use it instead as a call to dwell more intentionally within the wisdom of God revealed as its gift. Each day of this liturgical season, read at least one chapter from the Old or New Testament and deepen your friendship with God.

DAY 9

He who loveth Me, will be loved by My Father" [John 14; 21]. This at first sight seems absurd. For does God love us because we love Him? Far be it! Hence it is written in 1 John 4:10, "Not as though we had God, but because he hath first loved us." It must be remembered therefore, that anyone who loves Christ is not loved because he loves but because he was first loved by the Father. Therefore, we love the Son because the Father loves us. For true love has this quality, that it draws the love of the lover. "Yea, I have loved thee with an everlasting love, therefore have I drawn thee, taken pity on thee" (Jeremiah 31:3). But the love of the Father is not separate from the love of the Son, for it is the same love for both Divine Persons....God loves those unlimitedly to whom he wishes every good, namely that they possess God himself; the possession of Whom is the possession of Truth, for God is Truth....God...truly and unlimitedly manifests Himself to those fortunate and blessed souls.

COMMENTARY ON THE GOSPEL OF ST. JOHN

The spirit of the Lord is upon me,
    because the Lord has anointed me;
He has sent me to bring glad tidings to the lowly,
    to heal the brokenhearted,
To proclaim liberty to the captives
    and release to the prisoners,
To announce a year of favor from the LORD
    and a day of vindication by our God,
    to comfort all who mourn.

ISAIAH 61:1–2

PRAYER

God of Truth, I can love as you ask because you first loved me. In the footsteps of your Son, I am to walk the earth manifesting the glory of my heart's possession of you, our ultimate truth. What is this truth, but an absurd mercy for the oppressed, a mad love for the brokenhearted, an unrelenting pursuit of justice, and an irrational compassion for those imprisoned? Lord, like you, make my mercy absurd, my love mad, my pursuit of justice unrelenting, and my compassion irrational.

CHRISTMAS ACTION

Catholicism is not a "Jesus and me" spirituality. There are no solo flights to sanctity. We bring our oppressed, brokenhearted, and imprisoned brothers and sisters with us. Today, say a heartfelt prayer for someone you know who is oppressed by a special burden, comfort someone who is brokenhearted, or reach out to someone who is emotionally confined.

DAY 10

*T*he names conferred upon some by God always signify some gratuitous gift from heaven…Now since this gift of grace bestowed on Christ was that through him all men should be saved, so, very suitably he was called Jesus, that is, Savior….

In all these names, the name Jesus, which implies salvation, is somehow signified. Thus when he is called *Emmanuel*, which translated means "God with us," the cause of our salvation is signified, which is the union of the divine and the human nature in the Person of the Son of God, through whom it came about that God was with us by sharing in our nature.…When he is called *Wonderful, Counsellor*, etc., the way and term of our salvation are pointed out, inasmuch as we are led by the wonderful power and counsel of God to the inheritance of a life-to-come where there will be perfect peace, that of the Sons of God under the sway of God himself. When it is said, *Behold the man, the Orient is his name,* this refers to the same as the first, i.e. the mystery of the Incarnation, in that *light rises in the darkness for the upright.*

SUMMA THEOLOGIAE

For a child has been born to us, a son is given us;
  upon his shoulder dominion rests.
They name him Wonder-Counselor, God-Hero,
  Father-Forever, Prince of Peace.
His dominion is vast
  and forever peaceful,
From David's throne and over his kingdom,
  which he confirms and sustains
By judgment and justice,
  both now and forever.
The zeal of the Lord of hosts will do this!

ISAIAH 9:5–6

PRAYER

Prince of Peace, in the power of your name is my peace. Today on this earth, I know an imperfect peace. But one day, when I see the light of your face, that peace will be perfect. Until then, hold me "under the sway of God himself," that with zeal, I might spread the power and peace of your name to all I meet, especially those in greatest need of the healing light it brings.

CHRISTMAS ACTION

The manifestation of God through the name of Jesus is a revelation that heals and brings peace. Who needs peace and healing today in your family or among your coworkers or neighbors? How can you not simply *bring* that peaceful healing, but *be* that peaceful healing? Look for and act on two ways to be a healing presence today—a bridge of peace—whether through a phone call, a face-to-face conversation, a thoughtful gesture, or an intentional act of kindness.

DAY 11

*S*alvation was to be through Christ and to apply to all sorts and conditions of men, because in Christ Jesus *there cannot be Greek and Jew, slave and free man,* and so forth. In order that this should be foreshadowed in Christ's birth, he was made known to men of all conditions, because, as Augustine says, *the shepherds were Israelites, the Magi were Gentiles, the first were near, the latter from afar: both hastened to Christ the cornerstone....* [T]he magi were wise and powerful, the shepherds, simple and lowly. He was also manifested to the just, Simeon and Anna, and to sinners, namely the Magi. And also both to men and to women...so as to show that no human condition was barred from his salvation.

The manifestation of Christ's birth was a sort of foretaste of the full manifestation which was to come....

As Chrysostom says, *The Magi came from the east, since faith first rises from where the day dawns, for faith is the light of the soul,* or because all who come to Christ do so from him and through him.

As Ambrose says, *The Lord's birth had to receive due witness, not only from young people, but also from the old and from the just,* whose witness also was more trustworthy because of their uprightness.

SUMMA THEOLOGIAE

When the angels went away from them to heaven, the shepherds said to one another, "Let us go, then, to Bethlehem to see this thing that has taken place, which the Lord has made known to us." So they went in haste and found Mary and Joseph, and the infant lying in a manger. When they saw this, they made known the message that had been told them about this child.

LUKE 2:15–17

When Jesus was born in Bethlehem of Judea, in the days of King Herod, behold, magi from the east arrived in Jerusalem, saying, "Where is the newborn king of the Jews? We saw his star at its rising and have come to do him homage." And behold, the star that they had seen at its rising had preceded them, until it came and stopped over the place where the child was. They were overjoyed at seeing the star, and on entering the house they saw the child with Mary his mother. They prostrated themselves and did him homage. Then they opened their treasures and offered him gifts of gold, frankincense, and myrrh.

MATTHEW 2:1–2, 9B–11

PRAYER

Newborn King, you show no partiality in your love for us. Young or old, rich or poor, educated or uneducated, you could not love us any more in the next moment than you do in this moment. But my witness wavers at times, Lord. I lose track of the real Star, caught up in becoming one myself. Help me to once again kneel before you like a little child and open my treasuries of time and talent on behalf of the work for which I was sent.

CHRISTMAS ACTION

Where and in what capacity can you offer your time, talent, or treasure to a worthy cause for one hour this week? Possibilities include volunteering, helping a person in clear need or simply giving the gift of listening sincerely and attentively to someone. Try to make the decision by the end of the day.

DAY 12

*T*he Son is not born out of nothing but out of the substance of the Father.…[B]eing Father and being Son and being born are literally true of the divinity. Now the difference between a true begetting, whereby someone comes forth as a son, and a making is that the second is brought about by the maker out of material outside himself; e.g. a carpenter makes a bench out of wood, but a man begets a man out of himself. Now even as a craftsman fashions something out of his materials, God also forms something out of nothing…but that with nothing else presupposed, God produces the entire substance. Were the Son, then, to come forth from the Father as emerging from nothing, the Son would be to the Father as the product made is to its maker. In its literal sense, the term "sonship" obviously cannot convey this meaning.…The Son of God, therefore, does not issue from nothing, neither is he made; he is simply begotten.

…The name "sons of God" for those who are made by God out of nothing is a metaphor based on their being in some way likened to him who literally is the Son of God. Thus, it is he alone who as the true Son of God by nature has as his name, "the Only Begotten."...Inasmuch as becoming like him others receive the title of "adoptive sons," the metaphor, so to speak, of "firstborn" applies to him.

SUMMA THEOLOGIAE

We know that all things work for good for those who love God, who are called according to his purpose. For those he foreknew he also predestined to be conformed to the image of his Son, so that he might be the firstborn among many brothers. And those he predestined he also called; and those he called he also justified; and those he justified, he also glorified. What then shall we say to this? If God is for us, who can be against us? He who did not spare his own Son but handed him over for us all, how will he not also give us everything else along with him?

ROMANS 8:28–32

PRAYER

Only Begotten One, you were begotten out of sheer, exuberant love. You are the firstborn of many beloved sons and daughters, also loved lavishly. Help me to be just as lavish in the return of my love to the Trinity by conforming my heart and mind to yours. Liken me to your image that what the Father loves and sees in you, he may love and see in me.

Christmas Action

We have been "adopted" as daughters and sons of God, who desires to give us everything and *has* given us everything. Take a quiet fifteen-minute break today and make a list of all that you have to be grateful for. Title your list: "Not Coincidental, but Providential." Put the list in a place where you will come across it often to remind yourself that all good comes from a generous God and is not mere coincidence.

PART III

~~~~~~~

Daily Meditation

Opening Prayer

Show me your ways, O LORD,
teach me your paths.

Glory be to the Father and to the Son and to the Holy
Spirit...

EXAMINATION OF CONSCIENCE

Spend a few moments reflecting on this or the past day.
Have your words reflected the love of Jesus Christ? In
what ways have you neglected to act out of love? Have
fear, anxiety, worry, guilt, or selfishness led you to speak
to someone unjustly or unkindly? Pray for those you have
treated unfairly, and ask God to forgive you as you now
forgive those who have acted against you.

FROM PSALM 25

To you, O LORD I lift up my soul.
Lead me in your ways, O LORD,
and guide me in your truth.
Your mercy and love are everlasting.
Pardon my guilt.
Walk with me in all I do.
You alone protect me and give me refuge.

PRAYER OF THANKSGIVING

You have created me in your image, God, allowing my life to be filled with more than I can ever hope or imagine. Your goodness pours out anew into each day, and my blood pulses with your redeeming life. In gratitude, I offer myself as servant to your Holy Word. In all I do, please help me to love others that your will becomes my own. Gracious and giving God, fill me with hope and the spirit of Christ's passion to live in the fullness of your grace.

BLESSING PRAYER

God of wisdom and truth, your servant, Thomas Aquinas, kept his eyes steadily on the light of your Son, Jesus. Guided by the wisdom of Saint Thomas, which unfolded from the Most Holy Trinity, I entrust to the Sacred Heart of Jesus my heart, mind, and soul—all I do and all I am—all my choices and actions, on this and every day. O merciful God, bless me with humility that I may know the saving truth that all good things come from your love.

Holy Mother, Font of Wisdom, pray for me.
Amen.

Sources and Acknowledgments

WORKS OF SAINT THOMAS AQUINAS

Commentary on The Gospel of St. John, trans. J. A. Weisheipl with F. R. Larcher (Albany, NY: Magi Books). Copyright © 1980 by James A. Weisheipl. (Current rights contact: Continuum Books, New York.)

Excerpt from the English translation of a conference by Saint Thomas Aquinas from *The Liturgy of the Hours* © 1974, International Committee on English in the Liturgy, Inc. All rights reserved.

God's Greatest Gifts: Commentaries on the Commandments and the Sacraments, (a translation of *De decem praeceptis* and *De sacramentis ecclesiae*) (Manchester, NH: Sophia Institute Press, 1992). Copyright © 1992 Sophia Institute. Used with permission.

Light of Faith: The Compendium of Theology, (a translation of *Compendium theologiae*) (Manchester, NH: Sophia Institute Press, 1993). Copyright © 1993 Sophia Institute. Used with permission.

Summa Theologiae. Vol. 1: *Christian Theology*, trans. Thomas Gilby, OP, (1964); Vol. 7: *Father, Son and Holy Ghost*, trans. T. C. O'Brien (1976); Vol. 34: *Charity*, trans. R. J. Batten, OP (1975); Vol. 39: *Religion and Worship*, trans. Kevin D. O'Rourke, OP (1964); Vol. 48: *The Incarnate Word*, trans. R. J. Hennessey, OP (1976); Vol. 52: *The Childhood of Christ*, trans. Roland Potter, OP (1972); multi-volume work published by Blackfriars in conjunction with McGraw-Hill, New York and Eyre & Spottiswoode, London. Reprinted with permission of Cambridge University Press.

The Three Greatest Prayers: Commentaries on the Lord's Prayer, the Hail Mary, and the Apostles' Creed, (a translation of Reginald of Piperno's Latin summaries of Thomas Aquinas's three groups of sermons during Lent 1273) (Manchester, NH: Sophia Institute Press, 1990). Copyright © 1990 Sophia Institute. Used with permission.